SOCCER RULES THE WORLD

Hi, pleased to meet you.

We hope you enjoy our book about soccer!

I'm **VARbot** with all the facts and stats!

W

WELBECK

SIMON   DAN

Published in 2023 by Welbeck Children's Limited
part of the Welbeck Publishing Group
Based in London and Sydney
www.welbeckpublishing.com
Text © 2023 Simon Mugford
Design & Illustration © 2023 Dan Green
ISBN: 978-1-80453-512-7

Writer: Simon Mugford
Designer and Illustrator: Dan Green
Design Manager: Sam James
Commissioning Editor: Suhel Ahmed
Production: Arlene Alexander
Research Assistant: Eleanor Reid

Printed in the UK
10 9 8 7 6 5 4 3 2 1

Statistics and records correct as of December 2022

SOCCER SUPERSTARS

SOCCER RULES THE WORLD

SIMON MUGFORD   DAN GREEN

CONTENTS

INTRODUCTION

Are you one of the **BILLIONS** of people in the world who loves the world's **NUMBER ONE** sport?

If you are, then this is **DEFINITELY** the book for you!

SOCCER RULES THE WORLD brings you the most incredible stories about the **BIGGEST GAME** on the planet . . .

From *pioneering players* and the *greatest ever goals* to the *most magnificent matches* in history, welcome to . . .

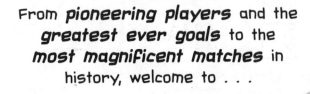

SOCCER RULES THE WORLD!

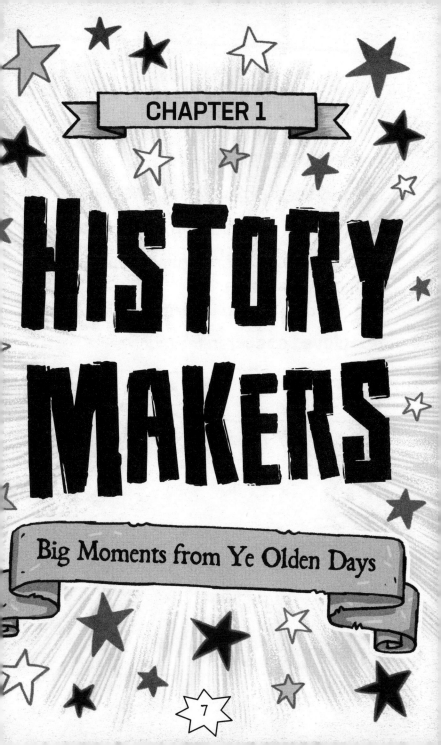

CHAPTER 1

HISTORY MAKERS

Big Moments from Ye Olden Days

THE CHRISTMAS TRUCE

December 25, 1914—the first Christmas of **World War I.** On that day, so it is said, thousands of British and German soldiers called a truce and the fighting stopped.

Instead, they shared food and drink, told jokes, and **played soccer** in the mud.

There are stories of an organized match, which the Germans won **3-2**, but the history books say this probably didn't happen.

But even if the soldiers only just kicked about a ball, it shows that sometimes soccer is much **more than a game.**

LEGENDARY LADIES

Dick, Kerr Ladies was a women's soccer team from **Preston, England.** They were formed at a factory in 1917 and played against both men's and women's teams.

The team gained a **huge following,** and in 1920, they played St Helen's Ladies in front of **53,000 fans** at Everton's Goodison Park.

This record crowd for a women's game stood for **98 years.**

It was a **charity match** to raise money for **injured soldiers** returning from World War II. The Dick, Kerr Ladies won the match **4-0!**

A year later, the English **FA BANNED** women from playing soccer!

UNBELIEVABLE!

11

READ MORE ABOUT THIS ON **PAGE 46**

THE 1950 WORLD CUP "FINAL"

The deciding match of the **1950 World Cup** saw tournament hosts **Brazil** (the favorites) play their South American rivals **Uruguay.**

Instead of *TWO* teams in a final, *FOUR* teams played a final group stage. This was the last match for both teams. Yes—*it's weird.*

The match was played at the famous Maracana Stadium in Rio de Janeiro. Officially, **173,850 fans** came to watch, but it's said there were up to **220,000.**

It was the largest ever crowd at a soccer match.

Brazil stormed through the tournament and they were the runaway favorites. But guess what? **Uruguay won . . . 2–1.**

ALCIDES GHIGGIA

This was Uruguay's **second** World Cup win—they had won the **first** ever tournament in **1930.**

PELE RULES!

NAME: Edson Arantes do Nascimento

DATE OF BIRTH: October 23, 1940

NATIONAL TEAM: Brazil

CLUBS: Santos, New York Cosmos

POSITION: Forward

More commonly known as Pele, **the 17-year-old** wonderkid scored a hat trick for Brazil in the semifinal of the 1958 World Cup. In the final, he scored two **SENSATIONAL** goals to bring Brazil their **first World Cup.**

A legend was born . . .

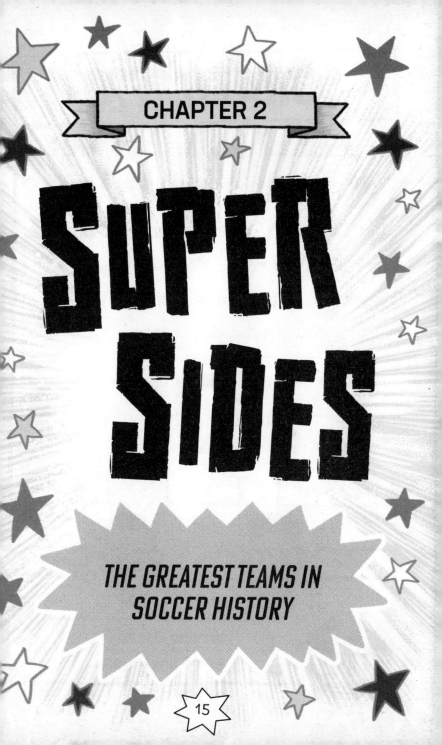

CHAPTER 2

SUPER SIDES

THE GREATEST TEAMS IN SOCCER HISTORY

BRAZIL 1970

The **Brazil** team that won the **1970 World Cup** in Mexico is often said to be the best ever.

Carlos Alberto, Tostao, Rivelino, Jairzinho, and, of course, **Pele** are some of the legendary names in a side famous for their beautiful, attacking soccer.

CARLOS ALBERTO

TOSTAO

RIVELINO

JAIRZINHO

PELE

Jairzinho scored in every Brazil game in Mexico.

16

Nicknamed The *Selecao,* Brazil beat every team they played at the tournament, including reigning champions **England,** to reach the final where they beat **Italy** 4-1.

It was Pele's **THIRD** World Cup win—the only player ever to do it.

Read about Carlos Alberto's famous goal in the final on page 76.

LIVERPOOL 1983-84

This Liverpool side made history as they became the first English team to win a **TRIPLE**:

The **LEAGUE** title (the **fifteenth** time)

The **League Cup** (beat local rivals Everton in the final)

Their **FOURTH EUROPEAN CUP**

Striker **Ian Rush** scored an awesome **47 goals** in all competitions in that season.

18

MANCHESTER UNITED
1998-99

Led by manager **Alex Ferguson**, this United team, which included **David Beckham**, **Roy Keane**, and **Ole Gunnar Solksjaer**, are the **only** English side to win the trip of the **Premier League**, **FA Cup**, and **Champions League**.

ALEX FERGUSON

SEE PAGE 60

The team went unbeaten in **33** games and the Champions League final against **Bayern Munich** is one of the most famous games in history.

19

DAVID BECKHAM

THE GALACTICOS

Starting in 2000, **Real Madrid** signed some of the finest, **MOST EXPENSIVE** soccer players in the world. They were known as the **GALACTICOS** and included:

LUIS FIGO, *WINGER*
€62 MILLION

ZINEDINE ZIDANE, *MIDFIELDER*
€73.5 MILLION

RONALDO, *STRIKER*
€45 MILLION

DAVID BECKHAM, *WINGER*
€37.5 MILLION

KAKA, *MIDFIELDER*
€67 MILLION

KARIM BENZEMA, *STRIKER*
€30 MILLION

CRISTIANO RONALDO, *FORWARD*
€94 MILLION

LUKA MODRIC, *MIDFELDER*
€32 MILLION

GARETH BALE, *WINGER*
€100 MILLION

NETHERLANDS 1974

This Dutch side played a system called **TOTAL SOCCER,** where each outfield player in the side, including the genius **Johan Cruyff,** would play in any position. It was quick, smart, and amazing to watch.

The team beat both **Argentina** and **Brazil** at the **1974 World Cup** but were ultimately beaten by a ruthless **West Germany.**

BARCELONA 2008-09

PEP GUARDIOLA

Manager **Pep Guardiola** brought his own version of **Total Soccer** to Barcelona. The star-studded side, including **Lionel Messi, Samuel Eto'o, Xavi,** and **Andres Iniesta,** passed the ball and moved quickly—they called it **TIKI TAKA.**

It worked, and Pep led Barca to the **TRIPLE** in his first season in charge and a total of **14 TROPHIES** in four seasons.

KA-POW!

MESSI RULES!

NAME: Lionel Andres Messi Cuccittini

DATE OF BIRTH: June 24, 1987

NATIONAL TEAM: Argentina

CLUBS: Barcelona, Paris Saint Germain

POSITION: Forward

*While at Barcelona from the age of 13 to 33, Messi won La Liga **10** times and the Champions League*

***4** times, as well as the **Ballon d'Or** a record **7** times. Known by many as the G.O.A.T (Greatest of All Time), Messi is the most gifted player of his generation.*

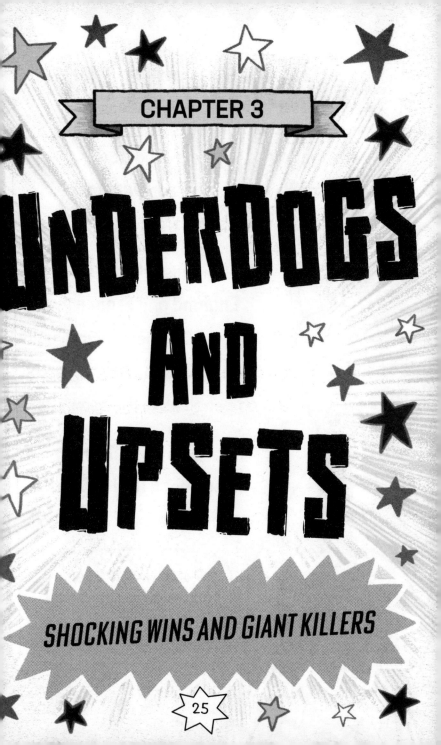

CHAPTER 3

UNDERDOGS AND UPSETS

SHOCKING WINS AND GIANT KILLERS

25

DANES CRASH THE EUROS

When Yugoslavia were expelled from **EURO 1992** because of a war, **Denmark** were the last-minute replacement.

After finishing ahead of **England** and **France** in their group, Denmark beat reigning champions the **Netherlands** on penalties in the semifinal.

Their 2-0 win over **Germany** in the final **STUNNED** the world of soccer.

> Probably the best tournament upset in the world!

SAUDIS SHOCK ARGENTINA

Argentina began the **2022 World Cup** as one of the favorites. Unbeaten in 32 matches and led by the magic of Messi, they opened their tournament against **Saudi Arabia** (ranked 51 in the world).

Argentina went ahead with a Messi penalty early on. But, in the second half, the Saudis scored TWO quick goals to produce a **WORLD CUP SHOCKER!**

Despite this shocking upset, **Argentina** went on to **win** the tournament (see page 70)!

FOXES RULE!

Leicester City were almost relegated from the **Premier League** in 2015 and began the next season as favorites to go down. But . . .

With a team of unlikely stars, including former nonleague striker **Jamie Vardy,** their Premier League win in 2016 is one one of the greatest upsets in all sport—not just soccer.

BOP!

TV's Match of the Day host (and Leicester fan) **Gary Lineker** promised he would present the show in his boxer shorts if Leicester won the league—and he did!

No pants!

VIKINGS SLAY ENGLAND

What happened when the stars of **England** came up against **Iceland** (ranked 34 in the world at the time) at **EURO 2016?**

England went ahead with an early penalty, but the Icelanders took advantage of a terribly **disappointing team** and won **2-1.**

SKOL!

WIGAN STUN CITY

With superstars, such as **Sergio Aguero** and **Yaya Toure,** in their team, City were the favorites to beat Wigan in the **2013 FA Cup Final.**

AGUERO

TOURE

With City down to 10 men, Wigan's **Ben Watson** headed in a ninety-first-minute winner.

UNBELIEVABLE SCENES!

The following week, Wigan were relegated from the Premier League.

JOY FOR JAPAN

In March 2011, Japan was struck by a terrible **tsunami** that killed thousands of people. So the people at home did not pay much attention to their women's team at the **World Cup** in Germany. They had bigger things to think about.

A **MAGNITUDE 9** EARTHQUAKE HAS STRUCK JAPAN.

NEWS

DISASTER!

WORLD NEWS
LIVE

But the team were **AWESOME** and against the odds, they reached the final. After a tight 2-2 draw, Japan beat the **world's best team**— the **USA**—on penalties. It was a major upset and fantastic for the people of Japan.

Japan's **Homare Sawa** won the **Golden Boot** for being top scorer and the **Golden Ball** for best player.

HENRY RULES!

NAME: Thierry Daniel Henry

DATE OF BIRTH: August 17, 1977

NATIONAL TEAM: France

CLUBS: Monaco, Juventus, Arsenal, Barcelona, New York Red Bulls

POSITION: Striker

*Arsenal's all-time **top scorer** and Premier League legend, as well as **triple winner** with Barcelona and a **World Cup** and **EUROs winner** with France, Thierry Henry is one of the finest strikers of all time to play the game.*

CHAPTER 4

MEGA MANAGERS

THE BEST BRAINS IN THE GAME

ALEX FERGUSON

"Fergie" led **Manchester United** for an astonishing 27 years. He made stars out of youth team players, such as **David Beckham** and **Paul Scholes,** and signed major talents, including **Roy Keane** and **Cristiano Ronaldo,** to bring unmatched success to United. He's probably the greatest manager of all time.

13 PREMIER LEAGUE TITLES

5 FA CUPS

2 CHAMPIONS LEAGUE TITLES

SHANKLY *AND* PAISLEY

In the 1960s, **Bill Shankly** transformed **Liverpool** from Second Division's loss cause to **three-time** First Division champions, as well as FA Cup and UEFA Cup winners.

BILL SHANKLY

BOB PAISLEY

Shankly's assistant **Bob Paisley** took over in 1974 and won **SIX** more league titles and **THREE** European Cups. **Liverpool legends.**

BRIAN CLOUGH

Clough led **Derby County** to a First Division title in 1972, then did the same at **Nottingham Forest** in 1978, having just got them promoted. But that's not all . . .

Having qualified for the **European Cup,** Clough's Forest **WON** it back-to-back in **1979** and **1980**.

In 1979, Clough famously signed Great Britain's first **£1 MILLION** player: **Trevor Francis.**

"*I WOULDN'T SAY I WAS THE BEST MANAGER IN THE BUSINESS. BUT I WAS IN THE* **TOP ONE.**"

ARSENE WENGER

In 22 years as **Arsenal** manager, Wenger won seven **FA Cups** and three **Premier League** titles, including the **DOUBLE** twice.

Wenger's "scientific" approach to soccer earned him the nickname "Le Prof" and his influence on modern soccer is **HUGE.**

CARLO ANCELOTTI

It takes a lot to beat **"Don Carlo."** He's won FOUR **Champions Leagues** as a manager—more than anyone else—and is the only boss to win each of Europe's **top five** leagues.

OTTO REHHAGEL

An underdog specialist, Rehhagel twice won the **Bundesliga** with **Werder Bremen** and then with **Kaiserslautern**— having just won promotion! But his shock triumph— winning **EURO 2004** with Greece—tops them all.

ALF RAMSEY

Tracto Boys foreve

Ramsey won **Ipswich Town** promotion from the old **Second Division** in 1961. Incredibly, the Suffolk club were English champions the following season and Ramsey left to manage **England.**

Winning the **1966 World Cup** makes Alf Ramsey one of the most celebrated English managers of all time.

JURGEN KLOPP

Klopp's style of exciting, attacking soccer has won Liverpool both the **Champions League** and the **Premier League** and a new generation of fans. A modern-day master.

SARINA WIEGMAN

By leading the England women's team to victory in **EURO 22,** she's won a place in the heart of every England fan.

BEST RULES!

NAME: George Best

DATE OF BIRTH: May 22, 1946

NATIONAL TEAM: Northern Ireland

CLUBS: Manchester United *(and many others, including Fulham)*

POSITION: Winger, attacking midfielder

*Famous for his long hair and cool clothes, Best was the original **fashionable soccer player**. The **Manchester United** star of the 1960s and 70s was the most **dazzling** player of the time—with his dribbling, passing, and scoring skills, he was **unstoppable**.*

CHAPTER 5

WOMEN RULE

45

FREE TO PLAY

Despite the success of the sport, especially in the late **1910s**, the FA believed that soccer was bad for women—no one knows why—so women's soccer was officially **BANNED** from **1921** to **1970**. It was also banned in **Brazil** and **Germany**.

In England, **Southampton Women** won the

first women's **FA Cup Final** in **1971.** Their star player, **Pat "Thunder" Davies,** scored a hat trick and they beat **Stewarton Thistle** 4-1.

Southampton would go on to win the FA Cup **seven** more times.

Davies was later selected for England Women when they played their first international match against **Scotland** in 1972.

GO USA!

The first **FIFA Women's World Cup** was held in China in **1991.** It was won by the **USA**—and they went on to win again in **1999, 2015,** and **2019.** They have produced some of the **BIGGEST** names in women's soccer.

MIA HAMM

POSITION: **FORWARD**

YEARS: **1989-2004**

158 goals in **276 games**

MEGAN RAPINOE

POSITION: **MIDFIELDER**

YEARS: **2005-PRESENT**

Ballon d'Or winner **2019**

CARLI LLOYD

POSITION: **FORWARD**

YEARS: **1999-2021**

Scored a famous **hat trick** in the **2015** World Cup final

WONDER WOMEN

Here are some more star names in the women's game to look for:

SAM KERR

COUNTRY: **AUSTRALIA**

POSITION: **FORWARD**

YEARS: *2008-PRESENT*

Golden Boot winner in three different leagues

All-time top scorer in the USA's NWSL

Kerr is the only Australian—male or female—to score a **World Cup** hat trick.

WENDIE RENARD

COUNTRY: **FRANCE**

POSITION: **DEFENDER**

YEARS: **2006-PRESENT**

Won 14 French League titles

Won SEVEN Champions League titles

ALEXIA PUTELLAS

COUNTRY: **SPAIN**

POSITION: **MIDFIELDER/WINGER**

YEARS: **2010-PRESENT**

Won a TRIPLE with Barcelona in 2021

Voted FIFA Best Player in 2021

LIONESSES RULE!

England was the host nation for **Women's EURO 2022.** The year before, the men's team had reached a EUROs final **for the first time,** but they failed to win. Could the **Lionesses** beat that?

England faced **Germany** (their main rival) in the final at Wembley. **Ella Toone** put England ahead, but Germany equalized and the match went into extra time.

The attendance was **87,192**—a record EUROs crowd for men or women.

Chloe Kelly wrote herself into the history books with a goal at 110 minutes. England won **2–1**.

INCREDIBLE!

YES!

The match was watched on TV by **17.6 MILLION** soccer fans.

LIONESS *LEGENDS*

The 2022 England win made the players household names, such as:

LEAH WILLIAMSON

POSITION: **MIDFIELD/CENTERBACK**

CLUB: **ARSENAL**

England's awesome captain

CHLOE KELLY

POSITION: **STRIKER**

CLUB: **MANCHESTER CITY**

Scored the winner in the EURO 2022 final

BETH MEAD

POSITION: **FORWARD**

CLUB: **ARSENAL**

Won the Golden Boot
at EURO 2022

ALESSIA RUSSO

POSITION: **FORWARD**

CLUB: **MANCHESTER UNITED**

Scored a superb
back-heel goal in the
EURO 2022 semifinal

PARR RULES!

NAME: Lily Parr

DATE OF BIRTH: April 26, 1905

NATIONALITY: English

CLUBS: St Helens Ladies, Dick, Kerr Ladies

POSITION: Forward

*Parr was a true trailblazer, a **legend** in the history of the women's game. Playing for more than 30 years for the famous club **Dick, Kerr Ladies,** Parr had a powerful left foot and is said to have scored more than **900 goals!***

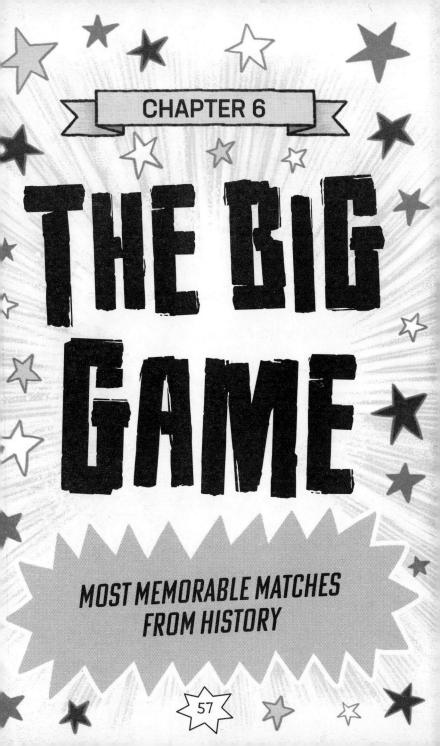

CHAPTER 6

THE BIG GAME

MOST MEMORABLE MATCHES FROM HISTORY

JULY 23, 1966

WORLD CUP QUARTERFINAL

PORTUGAL 5-3 NORTH KOREA

GOODISON PARK

North Korea had already produced the shock of the tournament—beating **Italy 1-0** in the group stage. Now they faced a **Portugal** side with the great **Eusebio** in the quarterfinal.

Incredibly, North Korea went ahead just after **KICKOFF**, and were 3-0 up after just 25 minutes!

BOOM!

Eusebio suddenly took charge, scoring FOUR GOALS—including two penalties— before **Jose Augusto** made it five.

UNBELIEVABLE!

More than **100,000** fans had gathered in the heat of **Mexico City** to watch two soccer giants.

Italy led early on, only for **West Germany** to equalize in stoppage time. What followed was the most extraordinary extra time ever:

94 MINUTES: GERMANY GOAL **1-2**

98 MINUTES: ITALY GOAL **2-2**

104 MINUTES: ITALY GOAL **3-2**

110 MINUTES: GERMANY GOAL **3-3**

111 MINUTES: ITALY GOAL **4-3**

Five extra-time goals, both teams exhausted.

Fans had just witnessed

THE **GAME** OF THE **CENTURY.**

MEXICO 70

PHEW, I'M EXHAUSTED!

ITV

MAY 26, 1989

FIRST DIVISION

LIVERPOOL 0-2 ARSENAL

ANFIELD STADIUM

Liverpool were three points ahead of **Arsenal** going into this game—the **First Division** decider. Liverpool were the title holders and had just won the **FA CUP.** They were THE team to beat. Arsenal needed to win by **TWO** clear goals to clinch the league on goal difference.

The *First Division* became the *Premier League* in 1992. This is the old trophy.

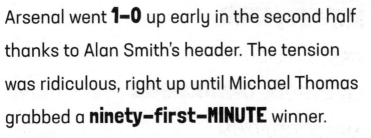

Arsenal went **1-0** up early in the second half thanks to Alan Smith's header. The tension was ridiculous, right up until Michael Thomas grabbed a **ninety-first-MINUTE** winner. **MAYHEM.** The Arsenal fans went wild! It was one of the greatest moments in Arsenal's history.

MICHAEL THOMAS

BOOM!

MAY 26, 1999

CHAMPIONS LEAGUE FINAL

MANCHESTER UNITED 2-1 BAYERN MUNICH

NOU CAMP, BARCELONA

Both teams went into this match as league champions. Manchester United were also FA cup winners. Win this and they would claim a **TRIPLE.**

Bayern Munich were ahead after just **SIX MINUTES**. United couldn't break through until David Beckham's **stoppage-time** corner found sub **Teddy Sheringham** . . .

GOAL! 1-1! Game on.

Instantly, United had another corner . . . **Ole Gunnar Solksjaer** (also a sub) was there to score!

UNITED WON 2-1!

The Bayern players were broken—while the United players and fans were in dreamland.

MAY 25, 2005

CHAMPIONS LEAGUE FINAL

AC MILAN 3-3 LIVERPOOL (AET)

ATATURK STADIUM, ISTANBUL

Liverpool were the underdogs against a peak **AC Milan**. And the Italian side went ahead in under a minute. By halftime, Liverpool were losing 3-0 and it looked to be all over for **The Reds**.

But something incredible happened in the second half. Thanks to goals from **Steven Gerrard, Vladimir Smicer,** and **Xabi Alonso,** Liverpool made it 3-3, forcing extra time and a penalty shootout.

VLADIMIR SMICER

STEVEN GERRARD

XABI ALONSO

Liverpool keeper Jerzy Dudek was the hero as they won the shootout to cap an incredible comeback:

THE **MIRACLE** OF **ISTANBUL.**

JANUARY 10, 2010

AFRICA CUP OF NATIONS GROUP STAGE

ANGOLA 4-4 MALI

NOVEMBER 11 STADIUM

The opening game of the tournament saw host nation **Angola** go into halftime leading **2-0**, thanks to their striker **Flavio**.

They extended their lead to **4-0** in the second half, but Mali's **Seydou Keita** and **Frederic Kanoute** got Mali back in the game. It was **4-2** in the ninetieth minute, but then . . .

FREDERIC KANOUTE

Keita and **Mustapha Yatabare** added TWO more in injury time to produce a stunning fightback.

DECEMBER 18, 2022

WORLD CUP FINAL

ARGENTINA 3-3 FRANCE *(4-2 on penalties)*

LUSAIL STADIUM, QATAR

The holders France faced tournament favorites **Argentina** in what was billed as a showdown between **Lionel Messi** and **Kylian Mbappe.** And what a match it was!

Argentina dominated for **80 minutes** with a 2-0 lead. Then in a breathtaking final 10 minutes, **Mbappe** scored from the spot and quickly equalized with an incredible volley to force extra time.

Messi restored Argentina's lead, only for Mbappe's late penalty to take the game to the shootout, where the South Americans prevailed. **INCREDIBLE** scenes!

It was hailed as the

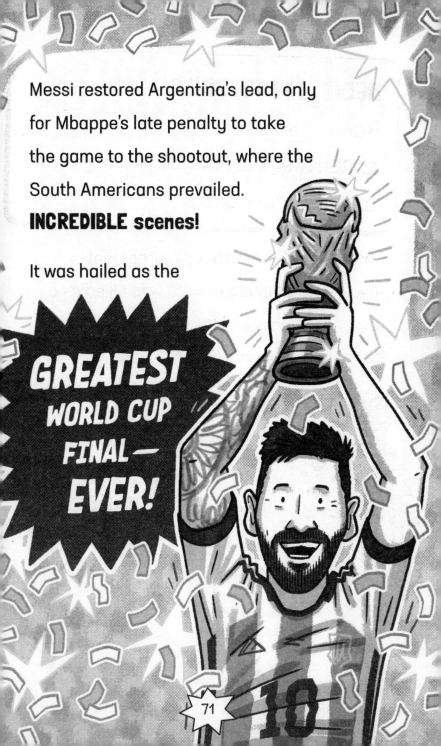

GREATEST WORLD CUP FINAL — EVER!

BECKHAM RULES!

NAME: David Robert Joseph Beckham

DATE OF BIRTH: May 2, 1975

NATIONAL TEAM: England

CLUBS: Manchester United, Preston North End (loan), Real Madrid, LA Galaxy, AC Milan (loan), Paris Saint-Germain

POSITION: Midfielder

*Probably the finest midfielder of his generation and known for his incredible **bending crosses** and **free kicks**, Beckham won **19** major trophies, mostly with **Manchester United**, and his fame extends way beyond the game.*

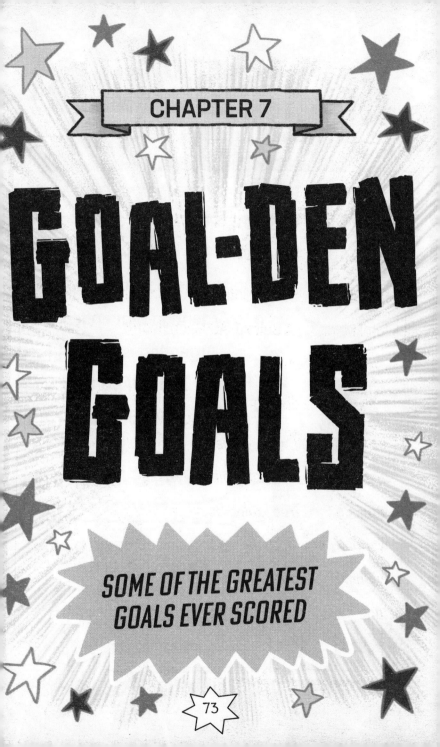

THE GOAL OF THE CENTURY

The **1986 World Cup** quarterfinal between England and Argentina that ended 2-1 to Argentina is remembered for **TWO GOALS** by Diego Maradona.

THAT'S HANDY!

Maradona is *hands down* one of the greatest ever players.

Even *hands up!*

74

Just **four minutes** after the ref missed his **handball** goal (the "Hand of God") and left England reeling, Maradona started a run in his own half. He swept past FOUR England players before sending keeper Peter Shilton the wrong way to score the *GOAL OF THE CENTURY.*

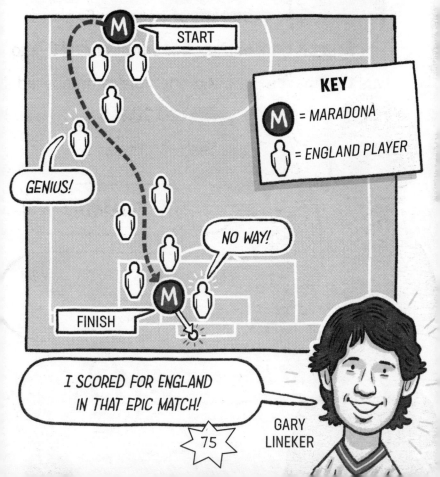

THE GOAL THAT MADE
BRAZIL

JUNE 21, 1970   BRAZIL 4-1 ITALY

The Brazil team that won the **1970 World Cup** was one of the **greatest** of all time.

The **fourth goal** in their **4–1** win over **Italy** was the finest example of their greatness.

KA-POW!

Brazil began a move in their own half, dribbling past the Italians and eventually finding their star forward **Pele.**

Captain **Carlos Alberto** had started a run down the right and, when Pele's perfect pass found him, he struck it amazingly: **_BOOM._**

ZOOM!

THE BEAUTIFUL GAME HAD ARRIVED!

MESSI'S MARADONA MOMENT

APRIL 18, 2007
BARCELONA 5-2 GETAFE

Back in **2007**, Barcelona's Lionel Messi was yet to become the legend we know. This goal, against **Getafe** in the **Copa Del Rey** semifinal, was *almost identical* to Maradona's Goal of the Century.

Messi picked up the ball *in his own half* and then dribbled past two players. Running at speed with the ball at his feet, he **zipped and turned** his way through three more opponents, and rounded the keeper to score.

AN INCREDIBLE SOLO GOAL.

Barcelona's fans voted this as the **BEST EVER** Barcelona goal.

ROONEY BIKES BACK

A bicycle-kick goal impresses on any occasion, but in the **Manchester Derby** it's sensational.

Wayne Rooney's 2011 effort against City was one of the best—and most **spectacular**—Premier League goals on record.

BLAM!

ZLATAN SINKS ENGLAND

NOVEMBER 14, 2012   SWEDEN 4-2 ENGLAND

Sweden's **Zlatan Ibrahimovic** was already on a hat trick, when from **way outside the box** and with his back to goal, his acrobatic **bicycle kick** sent the ball flying into the **England** net.

TAKE ZLAT!

81

RONALDO'S PORTO PILE DRIVER

APRIL 15, 2009   PORTO 0-1 MANCHESTER UNITED

In **2009**, **Manchester United** were in Portugal, playing **Porto** away in the **Champions League** quarterfinal. United needed to win or they would be out of the competition. Only **six** minutes into the game, Cristiano Ronaldo picked up a pass from **40** yards out and **fired . . .**

WHOMP!

It was a real screamer, flying at **64.2 miles per hour,** and . . .

The Porto keeper had **no chance!**

THIS WAS THE **BEST** GOAL I EVER SCORED!

RONALDO RULES!

NAME: Cristiano Ronaldo dos Santos Aveiro

DATE OF BIRTH: February 5, 1985

NATIONAL TEAM: Portugal

CLUBS: Sporting Lisbon, Manchester United (2003-2009), Real Madrid, Juventus, Manchester United (2021-2022), Al Nassr

POSITION: Forward/left winger

*The stats tell you everything about Cristiano Ronaldo. The **five-times Champions League** winner has more **goals, appearances, and assists** in the competition than any other player and the most international goals. He says he is the greatest of all time. Can you argue with that?*

CHAPTER 8

GAME CHANGERS

THE PLAYERS THAT HAVE MADE A DIFFERENCE ON—AND OFF—THE FIELD

BREAKING **BARRIERS**

Arthur Wharton is thought to be the **world's first black professional soccer player.** Back in the **1880s**, this sporting wonder (Arthur was also a track athlete and the fastest man in Great Britain) played as a goalkeeper and a winger for teams including **Preston North End** and **Sheffield United**.

In **1925,** Plymouth Argyle's **Jack Leslie** became the first black player to be selected for England. But when the FA realized he was black, they stopped him playing. **Unbelievable!**

Jack was finally awarded his cap in 2022, **34 years** after his death.

It wasn't until **1978** that England had its first full international black player, defender **Viv Anderson.**

Andrew Watson, who played for **Scotland** in the **1880s**, is thought to be the first black soccer player to play internationally.

MAGIC MARCUS

In 2020, **Marcus Rashford** was best known as an amazing forward for **Manchester United** and England.

But that all changed during the **Coronavirus pandemic.** When the British government planned to stop giving poorer families help with food vouchers, **Marcus spoke out.**

Remembering his own childhood, when his **family struggled for money,** Rashford started a campaign asking the government to change its mind.

And it did!

Social media lit up with love for Rashford. He was a soccer player **AND** an **activist**— a national hero, too!

I ♥ RASHFORD

PITCHING IN

Bayern Munich's **Sadio Mane** has never forgotten his home village of **Bambali** in **Senegal**. He has paid for a school and hospital there and regularly sends money to every family in the village.

Former Chelsea legend **Didier Drogba** has a charity that helps children in his home country of **Ivory Coast**.

Mario Balotelli is known for some crazy antics on and off the field, but he's famously funded causes from **homelessness** to **animal charities.**

The one and only **Zlatan Ibrahimovic** gave money to fight **Coronavirus** in Italy.

"IF THE VIRUS DON'T GO TO ZLATAN, ZLATAN GOES TO THE VIRUS!"

UH-OH!

POWER **PLAY**

From the 1980s until the early 2000s, **George Weah** played as striker for top European clubs, including **Monaco, PSG, AC Milan,** and **Chelsea.** Weah was one of the great players of the time and won the **Ballon d'Or** in 1995.

BALLON D'OR

His home country **Liberia,** in West Africa, experienced years of war and terrible poverty. At first, Weah worked with **children's charities** and the **United Nations**, which led him into politics . . .

. . . and George Weah has been the **PRESIDENT** of Liberia since 2018.

A GREAT HONOR!

93

THE *GOD* OF *NAPLES*

In **1984,** the great Argentine player **Diego Maradona** joined **Napoli** in the southern Italian city of **Naples.** It was poor compared to the northern Italian cities, where their clubs, such as **Juventus** and **AC Milan,** dominated Serie A. Naples was lucky to avoid relegation.

94

Maradona changed that. He led Napoli to their **FIRST EVER Serie A** title in **1987**, another in **1990**, the **Coppa Italia**, and the **UEFA CUP**.

UEFA CUP

THE GOD OF NAPLES

Maradona grew up poor, so for the people of Naples, he was one of their own. They **WORSHIPED** him.

KING ERIC

Eric Cantona was a Premier League legend at England's **Manchester United,** but he was famously often in trouble. **Banned** from soccer for kung fu-kicking a Crystal Palace fan in **1995**, his **bad boy** style made him famous outside of soccer.

Cantona went on to become an actor!

GAZZA'S TEARS

When **Paul Gascoigne** received a yellow card in the **1990 World Cup** semifinal between **England** and **West Germany,** he started crying, because it meant he would miss the final if England went through.

His tearful reaction melted hearts around the world and he became one of the most **famous** people on the planet.

SNIFF!

But England lost on penalties.

THE **QUEEN** OF SOCCER

Marta is the arguably the greatest female player of all time—**Pele** himself named his fellow Brazilian **"Pele in skirts."** Marta has scored more **World Cup** goals than any player, male or female: **17.** Her superb skill has won her **SIX** FIFA World Player of the Year Awards.

PIONEERING POWELL

Hope Powell was a pioneering women's player in the 1980s and 90s before becoming the **FIRST EVER** full-time coach of the **England Women's team.** Having led England to the final of **EURO 2009,** Hope paved the way for the successful **Lionesses** today.

RuNALDO RuLES!

NAME: Ronaldo Luis Nazario de Lima

DATE OF BIRTH: September 18, 1976

NATIONAL TEAM: Brazil

CLUBS: Cruzeiro, PSV Eindhoven, Barcelona, Inter Milan, Real Madrid, AC Milan, Corinthians

POSITION: Striker

*Known as **The Phenomenon,** Ronaldo's style of playing up front—starting an attack deep and dribbling at pace—was a massive influence on today's strikers. At his best, there were few strikers better than Ronaldo.*

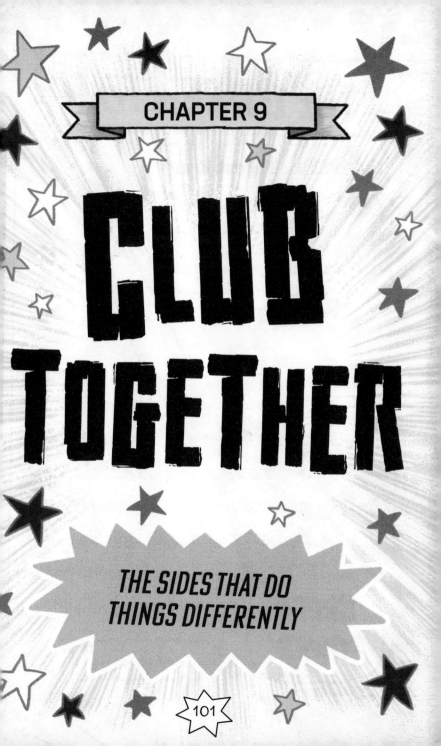

CHAPTER 9

CLUB TOGETHER

THE SIDES THAT DO THINGS DIFFERENTLY

THE GREEN TEAM

The **GREEN** in **Forest Green Rovers** is more than just a name. It is the world's most environmentally friendly club.

The **English League One** club is the only **VEGAN** club in the world. All the pies sold there are vegan, and the players take vegan packed lunches to away games.

GREEN POWER!

Nom, nom!

Their **organic field** is watered with **recycled rain** and **waste water,** and the team travel in an **electric coach.**

WHIZZ!

BEEP! BEEP!

ELECTROBUS

Barcelona defender and former Arsenal player **Hector Bellerin** is a major investor in the club.

HECTOR IS VEGAN

THANKS HECTOR!

SOCCER **ANARCHISTS**

St. Pauli is a club in **Hamburg, Germany.**
Their record on the field is unremarkable,
yo-yoing between the **Bundesliga** and the
German **second tier.**

But it's the **fans** that make the club stand out . . .

Since the **1980s,** St. Pauli has had a cult following of fans from the alternative scene of **punks, squatters,** and **radicals** in their city.

With their adopted skull and crossbones flag, the St. Pauli fans fight **AGAINST** fascist soccer hooligans but **FOR** social justice.

But still have a good time doing it!

EQUALITY RULES

Lewes FC, in West Sussex, England, is a club that likes to do things differently. For "The Rooks," **community** and **equality** comes first. Locals and fans are encouraged to own a stake in the club, where **pride** and **passion** is more important than **profit.**

Most important, Lewes is the first club in the world where the **men's** and **women's** teams are **truly equal,** playing with the same resources, funding, facilities, and support.

And their ticket sales, sponsorship, and performances are doing better as a result.

FANS FIRST

In **Germany,** soccer clubs must be partly owned by their fans. It's the **LAW! Bayern Munich**—the biggest German club of all—is **75 percent owned** by its **supporters.** Ticket prices are low and the fans have a say in how the club is run.

AMAZING!

STAR POWER

In the 1970s, the **NEW YORK COSMOS** signed global superstars, such as **Franz Beckenbauer** and **Pele.** The team suddenly became world famous, giving soccer (or football elsewhere) a boost in the United States. The team were more like **rock stars** than soccer players!

CUTTING *EDGE*

MLS side **Portland Timbers** have a VERY **unusual** way of celebrating a goal at their home stadium. The club mascot is a real-life **lumberjack, TIMBER JOEY.** When the Timbers score, Joey **CHAINSAWS** a piece of wood from a tree trunk for the player to hold.

TREE-MENDOUS *goal!*

BUZZ!

GOOD JOB!

109

CRUYFF RULES!

NAME: Hendrik Johannes Cruyff

DATE OF BIRTH: April 25, 1947

NATIONAL TEAM: Netherlands

CLUBS: Ajax, Barcelona, LA Aztecs, Washington Diplomats, Levante, Ajax, Feyenoord

POSITION: Forward/attacking midfielder

Three-times Ballon d'Or winner Johan Cruyff was the Dutch master of **TOTAL SOCCER,** the style of technical passing, movement, and positioning that revolutionized the modern game.

He is famous for the **Cruyff Turn**—faking a pass or shot before dragging the ball behind your standing leg.

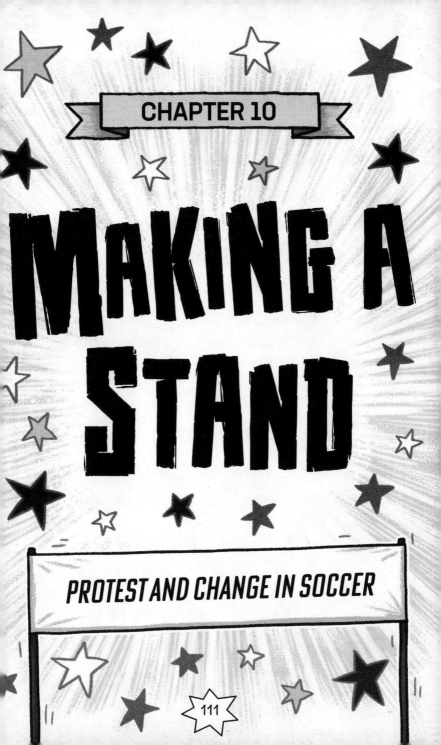

CHAPTER 10

MAKING A STAND

PROTEST AND CHANGE IN SOCCER

KICKING **RACISM** OUT

Soccer clubs, players, and fans around the world have played their part in speaking out **against racism** and other forms of **discrimination.**

The **KICK IT OUT** campaign led the way, starting in England in the 1990s.

Now, many teams choose to **take the knee** in a show of togetherness before kickoff.

WORLD CUP OF CONTROVERSY

The **2022 World Cup** in **Qatar** became known for much more than soccer.

"WHO WANTS A WORLD CUP IN WINTER?"

"IT'S TERRIBLE FOR THE ENVIRONMENT."

"IT'S ILLEGAL TO BE GAY IN QATAR."

"PEOPLE DIED TO BUILD THIS!"

"WORST WORLD CUP EVER!"

When **FIFA** told teams they could not wear a **ONE LOVE armband,** which promoted inclusion, the German soccer team protested . . .

FAIR **PAY**, FAIR **PLAY**

ALEX MORGAN

MEGAN RAPINOE

In 2016, players from the **U.S. Women's National Team,** including Alex Morgan, Megan Rapinoe, and Carli Lloyd, began a campaign to bring equal pay and funding to the men's and women's teams. In 2021, the **GOALS act** was passed, doing just that.

From **2022,** all players of both U.S. teams will receive the **same pay** for appearances and tournament victories, and **equal and fair** distribution of World Cup **prize money**.

CARLI LLOYD

ZIDANE RULES!

NAME: Zinedine Yazid Zidane

DATE OF BIRTH: June 23, 1972

NATIONAL TEAM: France

CLUBS: Cannes, Bordeaux, Juventus, Real Madrid

POSITION: Attacking midfielder

*"**Zizou?** is one of the greatest No. 10s ever to play soccer. **Elegant** and **stylish**, Zidane played with a vision and technique like few others. A winner of multiple titles and awards, including the **World Cup, Ballon d'Or,** and the **Champions League,** Zidane went on to be a hugely successful manager at **Real Madrid.***

TOP OF THE SHOTS

ALL-TIME TOP GOALSCORER
PELE (BRAZIL)
1,283 GOALS, **1,384** GAMES

TOP INTERNATIONAL GOAL SCORER (WOMEN)
CHRISTINE SINCLAIR (CANADA)
190 GOALS, **310** CAPS

TOP INTERNATIONAL SCORER (MEN)
CRISTIANO RONALDO (PORTUGAL)
118 GOALS, **196** CAPS

MOST GOALS IN A CALENDAR YEAR (MEN)
LIONEL MESSI (ARGENTINA)
91 GOALS IN 2012

MOST INTERNATIONAL CAPS (WOMEN)
KRISTINE LILLY (USA)
354 CAPS

WORLD CUP ALL-TIME TOP GOAL SCORER
(MEN AND WOMEN)
MARTA (BRAZIL)
17 GOALS IN 5 TOURNAMENTS

QUIZ TIME!

How much do you know about **SOCCER?** Try this quiz to find out, then test your friends!

1. Which team won the first World Cup in 1930?

---

2. When did Manchester United win the TRIPLE?

---

3. Which national side played TOTAL SOCCER?

---

4. Which team won EURO 1992?

---

5. Which team shocked Argentina with a 2-1 win at the 2022 World Cup?

---

6. When was the first Women's World Cup held?

----

7. Which player scored the "Goal of the Century" in 1986?

----

8. Who is believed to be the first black professional soccer player?

----

9. Which soccer club is the first in the world to pay men and women the same?

----

10. What is the Portland Timbers mascot called?

The answers are on the next page, *but **no peeking!***

ANSWERS

1. Uruguay
2. 1998/99
3. Netherlands
4. Denmark
5. Saudi Arabia

6. 1991
7. Diego Maradona
8. Arthur Wharton
9. Lewes FC
10. Timber Joey

SOCCER WORDS
YOU SHOULD KNOW

World Cup
The biggest tournament for international teams.

Ballon d'Or
The award for the year's best soccer player in the world.

Champions League
European club competition held every year. The winner is the best team in Europe.

Premier League
The top soccer (football) league in England.

Serie A
The top soccer league in Italy.

La Liga
The top soccer league in Spain.

Major League Soccer (MLS)
The top soccer league in the United States.

Euros
European Championship, Europe's main national team competition.

HAVE YOU READ ANY OF THESE OTHER BOOKS FROM THE SUPERSTARS SERIES?

SOCCER SUPERSTARS

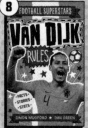

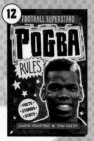

16 **ZLATAN** RULES

13 **DE BRUYNE** RULES

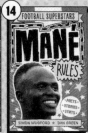

14 **MANÉ** RULES

15 **SOUTHGATE** RULES

HAALAND RULES

18 **MARTENS** RULES

19 **BRONZE** RULES

20 **LEWANDOWSKI** RULES

21 **GREALISH** RULES

COLLECT THEM ALL!

SPORTS SUPERSTARS

HAMILTON RULES

2 **RADUCANU** RULES

MORE COMING SOON!

ABOUT THE AUTHORS

Simon's first job was at the Science Museum, making paper airplanes and blowing bubbles big enough for your dad to stand in. Since then, he's written all kinds of books about the stuff he likes, from dinosaurs and rockets to llamas, loud musi, and, of course, soccer. Simon has supported Ipswich Town since they won the FA Cup in 1978 (it's true—look it up) and once sat next to Rio Ferdinand on a train. He lives in Kent with his wife and daughter, a dog, and a cat.

Dan has drawn silly pictures since he could hold a crayon. Then he grew up and started making books about stuff like trucks, space, people's jobs, *Doctor Who*, and *Star Wars*. Dan remembers Ipswich Town winning the FA Cup but he didn't watch it because he was too busy making a Viking ship out of brown craft paper. As a result, he knows more about Vikings than soccer. Dan lives in Suffolk with his wife, son, daughter, and a dog that takes him for long walks.